KING HAMLIN

A play by
Gloria Williams

Cover photo by Lara Genovese

Wordville

www.wordville.net

Naiad Productions & Freedom Tongues in association with Park Theatre presented the world premiere of KING HAMLIN at Park Theatre, London on 19th October 2022.

The original cast (in order of appearance) was as follows:

HAMLIN	Harris Cain
MAMA H	Kiza Deen
QUINN	Inaam Barwani
NIC	Andrew Evans

Writer/Producer	Gloria Williams
Dramaturg /Director/ Producer/Designer	Lara Genovese
Light Designer	Ben Jacobs
Sound Designer	Edward Lewis
Costume Designer & Creative Assistant	Elodie Chiper
Stage Manager	Melissa Berry
Graphic Designer	Shann Larsson

SPECIAL THANKS to Melli Marie, Sean Mathias, Anni Domingo and the Park Theatre team.

Supported using public funding by the National Lottery through Arts Council England www.artscouncil.org.uk.

SUPPORTERS:

Alt Africa www.alt-africa.com (Bespoke going out guide celebrating diversity)

A Fairer Chance (Reducing reoffending through employment)

A.S.I.P. (Adolescent Support Intervention Project)

The Bearded Butler (Sustainable Design and Build) www.thebeardedbutler.co.uk

Regis Road Recycling Centre

GLORIA WILLIAMS

WRITER & PRODUCER

Gloria is an award-winning playwright who is a graduate of The Royal Court Theatre Young Writers' Group and the Screen Institute. She wrote *Bullet Hole*, which ran at Park Theatre in 2018 and was shortlisted for the Alfred Fagon Choice award, won Best Actress at the Black British awards, and was shortlisted at The Off West End Awards for Most promising new Playwright. Her play *Monday* also garnered widespread acclaim and was performed at the Samuel French Off Broadway Festival at The Manhattan Repertory Theatre in Times Square. It also premiered in the UK at The Lost One Act Play Festival, winning Best Overall Production. Gloria was shortlisted for the Women Of The Future award in the Arts and Culture category, and has co-written the screen adaptation of *Bullet Hole*. *King Hamlin* won best full-length stage play at 2022 Scriptwriters & Co International Festival.

LARA GENOVESE

DIRECTOR, PRODUCER & DESIGNER

Lara is a director, writer, photographer and set designer with a degree in architecture. She directs, produces and set designs her own theatre shows and works in set decorating teams for studio feature films. She was a former Walt Disney imagineer-theme park designer in Hong Kong and an architect at Foster+Partners for two years. Her credits in London include *Bullet Hole* (Park Theatre) and several shows in Hong Kong. She is the director of the shorts *Frog*, *Nene*, *Kicking the Sky* and *Wow-er Woman*. Lara has co-written the screenplay adaptation of *Bullet Hole* which has now been optioned.

Cast

INAAM BARWANI

QUINN

Inaam trained at Theatre Royal Stratford East.

Some of his notable roles include: *Hidden* (Forest Forge Theatre); *The Boy Who Speaks in Numbers* (RADA); *Time Out* (Hooked Theatre) and *Listen* (BFI).

HARRIS CAIN

HAMLIN

Harris graduated from East15 Acting School in 2018 and has gone on to work on in TV, film and theatre.

Credits include: *Headliners* (SBTV); *Enterprise* (BBC 3); *Charlie and Stan* (Told by an Idiot); *Nothello* (Belgrade Theatre); *Simon Boccanegra* (Royal Opera House) and *Butterflies* (Tangled Feet).

KIZA DEEN

MAMA H.

Kiza trained at RADA.

Theatre credits include: *Rockets and Blue Lights* (National Theatre); *All's Well That Ends Well, As You Like It, Hamlet* (RSC); *The Phlebotomist* (Hampstead Theatre); *Random* (Leeds Playhouse); *Br'er Cotton* (Theatre503); *Expensive Shit* (Soho); *Trouble In Mind* (Ustinov Studio); *The Selfish Act of Community* (The Island); *Crave* (Young Vic); *Touch* (Arcola) and *My Life* (Warehouse).

TV credits include: *Hollyoaks, Young Wallender* and *Silent Witness*.

ANDREW EVANS

NIC

Andrew trained at Manchester School of Theatre. Since graduating he has worked as a puppeteer for Wild Rumpus. *King Hamlin* is his London stage debut.

Theatre credits include: *Cyrano De Bergerac* (Theatre Clwyd); *Winona* (Aberystwyth Arts Centre); *A Journey Through War* (Blue Orange Theatre) and *Incognito* (Manchester School of Theatre).

About Park Theatre

Park Theatre was founded by Artistic Director, Jez Bond and Creative Director Emeritus, Melli Marie. The building opened in May 2013 and, with four West End transfers, two National Theatre transfers and 13 national tours in its first nine years, quickly garnered a reputation as a key player in the London theatrical scene. Park Theatre has received six Olivier nominations, won numerous Off West End Offie Award, and won The Stage's Fringe Theatre of the Year and Accessible Theatre Award.

Park Theatre is an inviting and accessible venue, delivering work of exceptional calibre in the heart of Finsbury Park. We work with writers, directors and designers of the highest quality to present compelling, exciting and beautifully told stories across our two intimate spaces.

Our programme encompasses a broad range of work from classics to revivals with a healthy dose of new writing, producing in-house as well as working in partnership with emerging and established producers. We strive to play our part within the UK's theatre ecology by offering mentoring, support and opportunities to artists and producers within a professional theatre-making environment.

Our Creative Learning strategy seeks to widen the number and range of people who participate in theatre, and provides opportunities for those with little or no prior contact with the arts.

In everything we do we aim to be warm and inclusive; a safe, welcoming and wonderful space in which to work, create and visit.

★★★★★ "A five-star neighbourhood theatre." The Independent

As a registered charity [number 1137223] with no public subsidy, we rely on the kind support of our donors and volunteers. To find out how you can get involved visit parktheatre.co.uk

For Park Theatre

Artistic Director Jez Bond
Executive Director Vicky Hawkins

Creative Learning
Community Engagement Manager Nina Graveney-Edwards
Creative Learning Leaders Amy Allen, Kieran Rose, Vanessa Sampson

---

Development
Development Director Tania Dunn
Development & Producing Assistant Ellen Harris

Finance
Finance Director Elaine Lavelle
Finance & Administration Officer Nicola Brown

General Management
General Manager Rosie Preston
Producer Programmer Daniel Cooper
Administrator Mariah Sayer

Duty Venue Managers Natasha Green, David Hunter, Shaun Joynson, Leena Makoff

With thanks to all of our supporters, donors and volunteers.

Characters

HAMLIN KING, *Mixed Race Black/White-British, Male, 17*

QUINN, *Turkish-British, Male, 16*

NIC, *White-British, Male, 20*

MAMA H., *Black-British, Female, Late Thirties*

Setting

The play is set in London, 2021.

Locations

Outside a council home: front of house and terrace

Inside a council home: a very messy and cluttered living room

Derelict street area

Park

SCENE 1

A very dark room, young people fighting and then gunshots are heard.

A face is lit.

HAMLIN, *17, looks frightened and lost. He speaks to a* 'VOICE', *not visible on set.*

VOICE: Hamlin King?

HAMLIN: What? Where am I?

VOICE: Hamlin, have a seat.

HAMLIN: But I am already sittin'...

VOICE: Please tell me about yourself.

   A slight anxiety stutter begins.

HAMLIN: Bout myself? W-why?

   (beat)

   Hold on, it was today!? But I'm not r-ready though!

VOICE: So, tell me Hamlin, why are you looking for a job and what do you think you can bring to this company?

HAMLIN: I-I don't know.

VOICE: Where do you live, what part of town?

HAMLIN: North London? Does it matter tho? No? T-thought this was in a couple of d-days?

VOICE: One must always be prepared. Unfortunately, we feel you just don't fit the—

HAMLIN: Juss one question and d-dat's it!?

VOICE: Also, next time we hope you show up dressed properly.

HAMLIN: Huh? *(looking down)* I'm in my f-fuckin' PJs!?

VOICE: You were also not here on time.

HAMLIN: But nobody called me to let me know! I f-fuckin' would have been on time! This was too quick! Please, give me another c-chance! Pleeease!!!

HAMLIN's scream mixes with distorted sounds which continue to echo in the room.

Lights on.

HAMLIN breathes heavily, sweating and sitting up from the sofa in his tiny living room.

On the terrace of her council home estate MAMA H, *a woman in her 30s, peacefully waters some flowers and plants some sage seeds. She wears a colourful head wrap, though her hair looks like a mess. There is rubbish and clutter everywhere.*

It's late spring.

MAMA H: Jerome, Mark, and Dwayne… wish London could see more sun. God sends us only wind and rain.

MAMA H starts humming off key "Eyes on the Sparrow" while caressing some leaves. One stem breaks, MAMA H*'s heartfelt humming abruptly stops. She frowns and attempts to tie the broken plant to a stick.*

MAMA H: *(sighs)* Was never good at dis shit...

(beat)

My Nan use da tell me... *(mimics African accent)* 'All ya need is a lil talking and lil love". Huh...

MAMA H *looks are her sloppy result, not satisfied. She checks if her rescue 'surgery' is working, but the stem drops again. MAMA H takes a deep breath, determined not to fail. She grabs reinforcement plant tape and starts taping around the stem extensively.*

MAMA H: People be goin' half naked, *(tapes further)* lookin' marvellous, *(tapes further)* marvelling over everything. *(puts tape down)* Everything, except you. No one cares about you. *(placing tools away)* You can grow through the roughest weather and break free, you can make people laugh you knaw, you can make people cry. You can enchant with your sweet scent, but ya know what all people will see? Dem see your dirty stems.

MAMA H *acknowledges that her taping has turned out to be a complete mess.*

MAMA H:...and that you're still leaning a bit crooked to one side!

QUINN, *16, enters standing in front of* HAMLIN*'s house with a bag. In it are some paper cards, printed pictures of a teenage boy, coloured pencils and dead looking flowers. He sits on the low wall in front of the main door, dangling his feet and waving up to where* MAMA H *is.*

3

QUINN: Good morning, Mrs. King.

MAMA H: *(smiling)* Hamlin? Look who's here.

HAMLIN *rolls off the sofa, puts on the first pair of trousers he finds, tries to fix his hair, to no avail, and rushes outside in his wrinkled clothes.*

HAMLIN: Yo, Quinn!

QUINN: Yo… err, oh man, you look like morning. Got the stuff. *(hands bag over)*

HAMLIN *sits next to* QUINN *and pulls out two cards. They start writing on them.*

QUINN: Did you even wash your face, bro? You wreak of sweat.

HAMLIN: Had a lil nightmare, ok?

(pause)

I was at a job interview and…

QUINN giggles.

HAMLIN: Why you laughin' fam? I wasn't ready. I swear on my dad's life, I looked dat manager in her face, like I was God myself, and let her know dat I needed another chance bro.

QUINN: And what she say?

HAMLIN: I woke up…

(pause)

She askin' where I live!? Ain't say I live near them block towers.

(pause)

Dat went kinda tits up. Only a dream…

QUINN: *(serious)* The way they touch the sky always reminds me of the twin towers.

HAMLIN *gives him a funny stare.*

QUINN *looks at his scribble, not satisfied.*

QUINN: Yo, Hamlin, you… you ever wondered if Heaven has a ghetto?

HAMLIN: What kinda of question is dat? What like a hood up there or sumthing?

QUINN: Like a suburb on the other side or somethin'. It be shit ha! *(giggles)* Dem block of flats are like home to me.

HAMLIN: What? You're from another hood? You gonna cry over some ugly council flats now?

QUINN: I could always see them from my bedroom window. Like the first time I got my nuts wet.

HAMLIN: In the bath?

QUINN: No…

HAMLIN: Den why not put up a sign sayin' "Q got his dick wet for the first time here."

QUINN: Oh, shut up man…

The boys giggle.

HAMLIN: It's just steel, concrete and cheap windows. Am sure that when they blow those buildings down, they just gonna build sum new shit…

MAMA H: Hamlin? You got the stuff for Alex?

HAMLIN: Yeh Mum! We're making the cards now.

MAMA H: Good boy.

HAMLIN *picks up a couple of colours and draws something quickly.* QUINN *watches him draw with a concerned look.*

QUINN: Ham?

HAMLIN: Ha?

QUINN: Aww, you draw just like my baby cousin.

QUINN *take the colours off him.*

MAMA H. *comes down, still wearing her gardening gloves and trying to fix her hair.*

MAMA H: How are you, Quinn?

QUINN: Yeh, all good, I guess, Mrs. King.

MAMA H: Your mum still gonna sing at Alex's funeral?

QUINN: Yeh. She ain't sung in years. I heard her singing this morning though and, at her age, she can still do it.

MAMA H: Huuh?! Excuse me?

QUINN: *(chuckles)* Jokin' Mrs. King.

(pause)

It's weird, I can hear her heart in her voice.

MAMA H: We used to round u kids up in the nursery and she'd lullaby you to sleep.

QUINN: Nothin's changed, now with my new baby sista.

6

MAMA H: Aw, how is the new baby girl?

QUINN: Screamin' her lungs out all night…

MAMA H: Cute. But I don't miss that! *(winks at Hamlin)* I remember your mother would hold u up on her chest. Das all us mumz had to offer u boyz. A place to cradle.

QUINN: Yeh… Ehm, so…You lost weight Mrs. King!

MAMA H: Aww, and Hamlin don found it.

QUINN *chuckles.*

QUINN: Naw, he never found the weight, he ate it.

HAMLIN: Thanks Q…

MAMA H: Hamlin did you get the flowers?

HAMLIN: Yeh. Dey look kinda dead you knaw. Bad enough Alex's mum gotta 'Go Fund Me' for his funeral and now we putting dead flowers next to his casket?

MAMA H: Dead? God…

HAMLIN: Mum, relax. We're making the cards anyhow.

MAMA H. *frowns. She goes in the house.*

QUINN: She okay?

HAMLIN: *(lowers voice)* The kids at the youth centre ain't got food and their homes got split in two since the centre shut down. The Council Kingz want their buildin' back.

(pause)

7

She juss lost her job there… and now she gotta wait five weeks before she gets on benefits. Am not 18 yet so I can't get any too.

(beat)

Plus, her head is still hurtin' over my dad since last year.

(pause)

He was a good man. Juss too good for this hood.

QUINN: Yeah man… respect.

There is an uncomfortable silence.

MAMA H. *comes out again, this time with a pot of daises in her hands, a potted sage and some biscuits.*

QUINN: Custard creams! But where's the Baklava, Mrs. King?

MAMA H: You joker. You got Baklava money doh?

(pause)

Same old, same old.

QUINN *stuffs a biscuit in his mouth and then cleans his fingers on his T-shirt.*

MAMA H: Dese grew from the cracks in the street concrete. Always loved dem daises. Saved these before they tore down the building next door. Petals a bit damaged but you gotta give it to these little ones tryna get to the sun.

8

HAMLIN: Thanks Mum. *(grabs daisies)* I'll lay these with the cards.

(pause)

Hey mum? You placin' the sage pots out here now?

MAMA H: I need them. Gonna start burning dem leaves inside *and* outside. So, Hamlin, I need you to stop closing da windows *all* the time.

HAMLIN: No heatin'! So I gotta freeze my ass off for burnin' leaves?

MAMA.H: It's May?! No heating needed no more. Besides, they were Nan's favourite plants, so now they are mine and yours too… for good luck.

QUINN: *(munching)* I thought you were about to make some turkey stuffin'.

QUINN *grabs another biscuit and speaks with his mouth full.*

QUINN: Manz are hungry! *(chuckles)*

HAMLIN: You ain't serious.

MAMA H: It's family tradition. I'm tryna keep the bad energy out. If we close da windows and doors, you're just making it go dizzy. You got to let it out, so good can get in.

HAMLIN: Family didn't care 'bout you anyhow. So why have their cold shoulder breezing in here…

MAMA H: Stop it.

QUINN: Maybe we need sum of that in my mum's yard. Ya know, might get me a garden 'n one more room! We gettin' too many in there. Now with the new shoutin' thingy and my other sista lockin' me out. I dunno. My room had my spit DNA in the floor.

MAMA H: That's disgusting Quinn!

HAMLIN: Is that why you sleep on that tiny little sofa man?

QUINN: Yeh…

MAMA H: Well, I hope you get your room back soon Quinn. Then you can finally have somewhere to lay n rest boy.

(pause)

And hope you'll pull your trousers up one day. Boy, pull those up!

QUINN: What Mrs. King? It's my drip, ya know. *(chuckles)*

MAMA H: U need to find a job 'n getcha a new pair of drips that fits you. U had dem since three years now!

HAMLIN's *old looking phone buzzes in his pocket. He moves away, nearly tipping the food tray.*

QUINN: Heeey…

QUINN *quickly stuffs his mouth again.*

HAMLIN *looks at his phone. He frowns.*

MAMA H: No, please I can't—My heart can't tek this..

HAMLIN: *(faking it)* It's alright… another
   interview.

(pause)

   Mum?

MAMA H: I've been plantin' my sage pots real
   nice for u. Been prayin' you getta job soon.

HAMLIN: Mum, stop. Please stop worryin'.

   MAMA H. *holds* HAMLIN*'s hand.*

   QUINN *tries to lighten up the mood.*

QUINN: I'll just glue Alex on the front of a card
   and maybe…

   QUINN *begins to draw inside the card. He
   laughs to himself.*

HAMLIN: What?

QUINN: Naw nothin'.

   QUINN *shows* HAMLIN *the drawing. It is a
   cartoon portrait of himself.*

QUINN: In my mind I think I'm Idris Elba. I
   don't wanna know the truth.

   QUINN *crunches up the card and throws it
   in* HAMLIN*'s face. It falls behind some pots.*

HAMLIN: Fuck! Man! Now we have to make
   another one!

MAMA H: Hey! I didn't raise sum gutter mouth.

QUINN: Uff!

HAMLIN: *(embarrassed)* Sorry. *(to* QUINN*)*
   Hurry Idris. The funeral's gonna start soon.

   QUINN *starts making a new card.*

11

HAMLIN *picks up* ALEX*'s photo.*

HAMLIN: You remember when Alex used to fake a posh accent every time the police would stop him for no reason?

QUINN: Oh man. Every time he'd be like, *(RP accent)* "Officer how may I help you today."

HAMLIN: And the other time when he was the 'Lost Footballer.' "Mr Officer, I used to play semi-pro football for this country. That's right... I was once a hero!"

QUINN *and* MAMA H *giggle.*

(beat)

HAMLIN: Too much slashin' in dis hood. Bruddaz look like me and you. After each stabbin', you're like *wow*, den another stab and it's like *wow* again. How many 'wows' can you say in one lifetime? My minds gotta get used to it.

MAMA H: All my baby's blood in these streetz...

HAMLIN: At least Alex is gone from all dis Hell on Earth. At worst, he's just somewhere quiet, not a nothin'. At best he's an Angel. Why's that so bad? It's only bad for da people he left.

MAMA H: You mean like his mother...

(beat)

I gotta give you some money for the flowers you bought. *(gets up)*

HAMLIN: Don't worry about it. Quinn loaned me. I'll give it back when I get a job.

MAMA H: Oh Quinn, you Angel.

MAMA H. *exits.*

QUINN: Why did you lie to her?

HAMLIN: Shut up man! That text was another rejection. Couldn't tell her that. She came back from the Job centre cryin' the other day.

(beat)

Wanna good job, but ain't much out there at the moment and too many ask for workin' from home and dat shit is no good for me with no computer or wifi! I wanna be a software engineer but I ain't got the tools!

QUINN: Ham, chill, you juss a yout.

HAMLIN: Nah, I need to pattern up and help her pay off dese red letters somehow.

HAMLIN *holds back his tears.*

QUINN: I hear dat. Still.

(beat)

Bro, you know, I be tryna sleep, I keep seeing Alex in the light—like he's been singin' to me… *(sings out of tune)* "It's been a looong day, without you my friend. And I'll tell you all about it when I see you again…"

At first hesitant, HAMLIN *then tags along singing whole heartedly, off key. The two share the moment, laughing.*

HAMLIN: Bet he's waitin' with a new pair of trousers for you?

HAMLIN *chuckles.*

QUINN: It's embarrassing as fuck. I'm in year 11. I've grown a few inches. I gotta pull them down and walk around with my ass in the air. It's mad, my sister is growing so fast the teacher is on to her for her skirt being too short.

The boys hear NIC, *20, whistling 'baa baa black sheep' off-stage. They jump.*

QUINN: That's Nic, innit? I should shout at him.

HAMLIN: Let him go. Since Alex died, Nic thinks he's boss. You need to tell him he ain't no Superman.

(beat)

QUINN: Naw, he needs me.

Awkward silence.

HAMLIN: He *needs* you? What does he need a yout like you for! Bladez from da endz is after him. Since when do you follow Nic? You spend time with him now?

QUINN: Yeah…

QUINN *looks hesitant.*

HAMLIN: Go then.

QUINN: I'm gon.. Yo, Hamlin. I got something…

QUINN *pulls out some money from his pocket.*

HAMLIN: Don't need your money.

QUINN: Juss take it.

QUINN *hands the money and exits.*

MAMA H. *can be heard singing again.*

SCENE 2

The next morning. HAMLIN *walks in the living room where* MAMA H. *is picking sage leaves off branches. She looks fancy. The news is playing off an old small radio. The very crammed space is full of clutter and mismatched second-hand furniture.*

NEWS VOICEOVER: It's not just these areas of the city. We stand or we fall together. I'm here to ask for the chance to stand with you—

HAMLIN *turns the radio off, coming in with his usual wrinkled clothes and an undone tie.*

HAMLIN: Mum, I need help with my tie?

MAMA H. *does not answer, trying very hard to concentrate on her task.*

MAMA H: I'm preppin' my herbs, Hamlin.

MAMA H. *inhales the herbs' scent with a satisfied smile. A sudden sniffle arises. Confused, she slides the herbs away from her.*

MAMA H: Oookay right… uhm. Hamlin, I need to leave soon.

HAMLIN: What's with the fancy blouse?

MAMA H: U ain't the only one lookin' for a job.

HAMLIN: Please? I need to look slick for the next interview.

MAMA H: It's funny I stopped changing your nappies 17 years ago, boy…

HAMLIN *stares at her and puts on a puppy dog face.*

MAMA H: Oh, alright.

MAMA H. *smiles and helps.*

HAMLIN: What's up mum? Something wrong? Do I look funny?

MAMA H: Where's the rest of your clothes?

HAMLIN: I'll put dem on after.

MAMMA H. *giggles.*

HAMLIN *sways his head gently towards her.*

HAMLIN: What's the problem?

MAMA H: U gettin' old boy.

HAMLIN: What? I'm getting old!? Do I have white hair!?

(pause)

Well, then I'm getting wiser. You gettin' old.

MAMA H: Me seventeen years older than you. When I waz carryin' your little bum, you know how judged I waz by my mother and everyone? "Oh a black baby mum having a

16

baby with a white guy." Mum named a sage plant of hers after me and the day she kicked me out she cut its branches off… and us out of her life. But we were braver than all of them together, your dad and I.

(pause)

We stayed at my Nan's house for a bit until she died… and home was taken. Nan used to have dese plants all over her house. I watched dem grow 'n I grew to love them. She had a very special gift and it made me smile even in dese sad times. We were lucky cause later da Council gave us a home of our own and then we had you. It wasn't easy but we worked hard. Now half the women my age are havin' babies and my one child is almost out the house. I can officially retire from kidz, while still in my thirties.

See, I was smart.

HAMLIN: Mum, you joker.

MAMA H: Did I mention that most of them are twice my size, lookin' twice my age?

HAMLIN: One day my kidz will have the best lookin' Nan and people will think it's their mum.

MAMA H: I remember everybody was proper jealous. I had the nicest boy a gal could dream of. At school he'd give me a daisy every day. Would steal it from the school's garden.

HAMLIN: Here we go.

MAMA H: U remember summer milkshakes after school with dad?

(sings) "Summertime…"

HAMLIN: I'd get home and he left ice-cream so melted dat we ended up mixing up the chocolate and the vanilla.

MAMA H *giggles while she finishes his tie.*

HAMLIN *goes to stare at himself in front of the mirror.*

MAMA H: You knaw, when he was your age, he bought me my first mobile phone for my birthday. He had juss found a job at a local newsstand. We had you to look after. We weren't the richest people around, but we were the happiest.

MAMA H. *stares at* HAMLIN *for a bit with a teary eye.*

MAMA H: He was a good man. You remind me of him. My Hamlin King.

(beat)

HAMLIN: I donno…

MAMA H: U don't know?

HAMLIN *feels the pressure.*

HAMLIN: I donno… If they don't want me this time, who knows what I'll do.

HAMLIN *exits.*

The sound of mail dropping from the front door is heard.

MAMA H. goes to collect it. It's a Council brown envelope. MAMA H. looks concerned, opens it and immediately starts breathing heavily.

SCENE 3

Same day.

HAMLIN is dressed with a suit jacket, his T-Shirt, his tie and his wrinkled trousers. He stands centre stage. Besides him, a chair.

Lights on him. He looks very nervous.

On the other side of the stage sits an interviewer, played by MAMA H. She stares at HAMLIN, impassive.

The staging recalls Hamlin's nightmare earlier in the play.

INTERVIEWER: Hamlin King?

HAMLIN: Hamlin King, dat's me.

INTERVIEWER: Hamlin, have a seat.

HAMLIN sits.

INTERVIEWER: Please tell me about yourself?

HAMLIN: Sure, well... I'm studying for my A levels after recently getting As and Bs in my mock exams. Yeh dat's right... studying hard so I can transition to software engineering in the future. In the meantime, I would like to lend my services somewhere in a big retail store.

INTERVIEWER: Okay so why the application for this role?

HAMLIN: Why? I want to show young males in my community that hard work is still important in this current age of glamorized social media.

INTERVIEWER: That's inspiring Hamlin. Young people today may still forget that we all started somewhere. Keep going. Tell me a little more about yourself, your skillsets in relation to this specific role of 'Welcoming staff'?

HAMLIN: Well, over the years I've built up abilities and qualities that I believe are a match for any position you may have there, there on your list. I'm a positive thinker and I love being at work engaging with others and customers' needs.

INTERVIEWER: That's great. However, part of the job would require customer service online, so you can work from home. Would you like that?

HAMLIN: Well…

INTERVIEWER: It would help you so that you can do it right after school. Did you travel far today?

HAMLIN: What?

INTERVIEWER: Did you travel far?

HAMLIN: (*fidgeting*) Ah, no, no, just a quick tube. I mean I can come here, no problem. I prefer speaking to people face to face, if you know what I mean.

INTERVIEWER: Ok then, let's see if anything else in our other locations. What part of town are you from exactly?

HAMLIN: I uh…uh.

HAMLIN's *inner thoughts take over.*

INNER THOUGHTS: Again!? Dat a trick question? Does it matter where I live? You ain't gonna give me the job if I tell you. Also, I walked here. It's actually fucking far. Couldn't pay for the bus. I had to change my shirt coz wearin' a suit in my area is a bit complicated.

HAMLIN: …uh you know North… North.

INTERVIEWER: Yes, but what where?

HAMLIN: North ends, I mean…

INTERVIEWER: Am sorry, where?

HAMLIN: Alls I'm sayin' is—

INNER THOUGHTS: If u sound ghetto u won't get a job. 'Alls' is not plural. There's no such word as 'Alls'.

INTERVIEWER: Does not sound like you know where you live.

HAMLIN: Am… am from a good hood, I mean neighbourhood. Went to the best school and am r-ready to face the world.

INTERVIEWER: I see, that's pretty vague but—

HAMLIN: Oh okay… Dem block towers near the a…near the…station.

INNER THOUGHTS: Why u sayin' dat? Sound like ur a drug dealer now.

HAMLIN: I'm a fast learner you know! I'm a...
I'm a good listener. I-I like to guide people in
the best direction. My f-father always
thought me to be polite and so I know, oh I
know I am a good p-person. Oh, oh and I'm
very friendly, yeh. My mom's friends love
me and... and I'm very quick on my t-toes.

INNER THOUGHTS: Don't say dat. 'Quick'
means ur runnin' from da police.

INTERVIEWER: Okay, you sound a bit confused.
I am not sure we need—

HAMLIN: (*scrambling*) No, No!. Did...did...did I
mention my people skills? I... I... am great
at them and I wa-wa- want to learn more...
cause I feel it will help me for university.
Uhm yeh-uh yes, when I finish s-school I
want to go study. Well, I said that already.
Soooo, I am so happy I have this chance to
speak to you now to- to practice my people
thingy... s-skills... speaking? ... I need—

INTERVIEWER: (*writes something*) I see.

HAMLIN: Uhm, did I forget to mention how f-
fucking responsible I am!

The INTERVIEWER *halts.*

INNER THOUGHTS: You winner...

HAMLIN *hits his head again.*

HAMLIN: (*to himself*) Shut-up! Fuck off.

INTERVIEWER: Excuse me?

The INTERVIEWER *gets up to leave.*

INTERVIEWER: I think we've had enough for—

HAMLIN *stands up.*

HAMLIN: No wait!

(*pause*)

If anything is possible... do me a f-fucking miracle, open up the g-gates of Heaven and let me be a man! Give me another c-chance! Give me the job, p-pleeease!

Transition lights.

SCENE 4

Evening, same day. MAMA H. *takes the jacket off a tense and shaking* HAMLIN *who stands in front of the mirror, again. She folds the jacket and places it on a chair.*

HAMLIN: Feels like I'm dirty.

MAMA H: Excuse me?

(*pause*)

No.

HAMLIN: I look dirty... to employers.

MAMA H: You're my son. Who ever said that?

HAMLIN: Your son with no "skillset"...

MAMA H: But—

HAMLIN: ...or Wifi, or computer... can't even find a job myself online or F'n work from home

MAMA H: Hamlin!

(pause)

One day you'll be king of this world. But for now, keep tryn'.

HAMLIN: Every guy I know is mekin' money. Am tryna to get a decent job! I can't even t-take a girl out.

MAMA H. *crunches some sage leaves nervously.*

HAMLIN: It's like they see one celebrity on Instagram in a fine dining restaurant and that's the levels they want…

HAMLIN *takes a deep breath.*

MAMA H: You havin' sex?

HAMLIN: What? Muuum…!

MAMA H: I'm not ready for no grandkids. I ain't payin' for any babies. You can pay for them.

(pause)

Just be smarter than I was though. Degree first.

HAMLIN: You are smart, Mum.

MAMA H: All I ever and only knew waz some troubled kids. Wiv no fancy piece of paper I can only go so far… Been in the Council queue for a week. I then phone 'em, and they chargin' me with the sad violins playin' in da background. Hamlin, you need to look for sum quick option—

HAMLIN: But Mum—

MAMA H: Your dad used to do a few shifts at the supermarket. Nothin' to be ashamed of.

I will start too… though it's not enough. We both need to find good pay.

HAMLIN: Girlz will say I'm broke! Manz will take the piss outta me for not flexing on TikTok. Can't win.

MAMA H: Manz? Okay. Well, when u start havin' sum money, you can take a girl wherever you want.

(pause)

Juss never show up again to an interview with half your clothes.

HAMLIN *looks at her annoyed.*

HAMLIN: I can't!

MAMA H: You can't?

HAMLIN: I can't. I'll get the wrong eyes lookin' at me.

MAMA H: Hateful eyes.

(beat)

All this hate. When I worked in that youth club I knew deep, deep down in their hearts, these boys really don't wanna do half the things they do. They still be watchin' cartoon network.

(pause)

A boy wakes up, looks in the mirror, hates himself and then decides to kill another boy. I hate it.

HAMLIN: Coz his face ain't from the endz.

MAMA H: I know, but everyone's face is different.

HAMLIN: But it ain't juss the face, it's the hood dey walk in! This morning before my interview I thought death was standin' there to say hello. Sum boy looked at me like I ain't even black enough. I ain't black or white enough.

MAMA H: You are enough.

HAMLIN: But I looked different.

(pause)

He asked, "What you lookin' at?" and I'm like, "What am I lookin' at?" I think about his heart and I'm thinking is he lookin' at me? Or he's in pain. He thinks I see him and he don't want me to see his pain. So he puts on a shell of a tough person who's willin' to kill me because he's in pain. It's not like he wants to kill me.

(pause)

...he just doesn't wanna die.

(beat)

That's why I took my shirt off.

MAMA H: I see.

(beat)

I don't want you with no shell. Dat shell got your father killed tryna stop a fight of hateful eyes. God bless him dyin' for their sins.

A phone message ping is heard.

HAMLIN *looks down at his phone.*

MAMA H. *can see the screen over his shoulder.*

MAMA H: And…

HAMLIN *stays silent.*

MAMA H: You didn't get it, again…

HAMLIN: N-no…

MAMA H. *slowly goes to her sage, looking like she is about to collapse on a chair.*

HAMLIN *stands behind her.*

HAMLIN: I t-tried to get a good job mum. I really want to w-work!

MAMA H: I wish I could give you everything you want. I just can't do nothin' right these days… even dese stupid leaves…

MAMA H. *frantically ties fresh sage branches to hang for drying. Her tying is sloppy and her frustration worsened.*

HAMLIN: I'm sorry, I F-d up. I mean messed up—Maybe I should, dunno, see what people are up to dese days, in the area you know—

MAMA H: No! Tomorrow, you go to school and after you ask de shops here if dey need help.

HAMLIN: But I don't want—

MAMA H *gives* HAMLIN *a firm stare.* HAMLIN *gets the message. He exits.*

Transition lights.

27

QUINN *exits.* HAMLIN *crashes on the sofa hiding his face on the pillow.*

SCENE 6

Later in the week. Afternoon. QUINN *and* NIC *walk towards* HAMLIN*'s house with several boxes, struggling.* NIC *gestures for* QUINN *to stay behind.*

QUINN *objects and whispers loudly.*

QUINN: Oh, come on. I wanna ring the doorbell.

NIC: Shut up man! You'll juss fuck it up. (*stands in front of the door*) No! No! No!

QUINN: Nic, bro, you smell? You ain't showered? U should take one, mate.

NIC: Not as much as you need a nappy change.

NIC *smells his armpit.*

Ah, now that is how a real man should smell! Now sit!

QUINN *hides behind some rubbish bins.*

NIC *pulls up his trousers and tucks in his T-shirt. He goes to ring the doorbell.* QUINN *peaks from behind the bins.*

NIC: (*to* QUINN) I can still see you!

HAMLIN *opens the front door wearing cleaning gloves. He looks like a mess.*

NIC *chuckles.*

NIC: Look at you and your yellow gloves, Mr Muscle. (*grins*) Hey, cheer up! Who died this time?

NIC *pats* HAMLIN *on his head.*

NIC: Who's a good boy, who's a good boy?

HAMLIN *takes* NIC*'s hand away, annoyed.*

HAMLIN: Oookay, get off me. I ain't no dog, I dun smell like one.

NIC *looks him up and down.* HAMLIN *feels suddenly judged.*

HAMLIN: Err, you, on da other hand, smell like—

NIC: (*sniffing him*) You smells like milk.

HAMLIN: Huh?

(*tries to fix his look*)

Am helping mum clean up, so you gotta go—

HAMLIN *attempts to block* NIC *from entering.* NIC w*iggles his way in.* MAMA H. *enters, filling a bag with the trash spread across the room.*

NIC: Good morning, Mrs. King. (*surprised*) Do you need a hand?

NIC *takes his hat off and puts on a charming smile.*

Let me help u with dat.

HAMLIN: Whateva…

Annoyed, HAMLIN *exits.*

MAMA H: Ah! Lil baby soldier. Look at you and your manners. What, you can say hello now?

MAMA H. *quickly tries to make herself presentable. Her dark circles scar her face.* NIC *notices.*

MAMA H *goes to* NIC *and caresses his cheeks.*

NIC *frowns.*

NIC: Uhm. Nobody has called me that for years.

MAMA H: I know.

MAMA H. *struggles to give a smile. She goes to collect a toy from the table.*

MAMA H: Guess what I found?

MAMA H. *grabs a transformer toy.*

MAMA H: Was finding things to sell and stumbled on this.

(*shows toy*)

Got me reminicin' of u four boyz in the playground. When Ham was pullin' your hair. You keep it.

NIC: Uhm, no thank you Miss H, am a big boy now....

MAMA H: Don't be actin' like u never clung tightly to this toy when u would come to see me at the club. Am juss gonna keep it here. If you change ur mind.

(*winks*)

34

MAMA H. *places the toy on the table, pensively.*

NIC: Are u okay, Miss King?

MAMA H: Almost brought a tear to my eye, rememberin' Alex, Hamlin, Q and you pretending to sword fight in the mud. You boyz together in one safe place.

NIC: Yeah, we was a mess, we...

MAMA H: Bless, Alex's mother was always laughin'. She'd say: "if those boyz can walk through mud they can swim through blood."

(beat)

Ham always looked up to ya, you know?

NIC: *(proudly)* Yeah? You always helped me up da swing 'coz Mum... well, she waz busy.

(beat)

Till I never saw her again.

MAMA H: Talk to me sometime yeh? Please.

NIC: Thank you, Mrs., King.

(shouting to off stage)

Ham? Broski? I'll wait for you here when you're done.

MAMA H: Gonna go lie my head down. Don't you boys get into any trouble now.

MAMA H. *winks and exits.*

NIC *rushes to the door to whistle for* QUINN.

NIC: (*To* QUINN) Ehi!

35

QUINN *sits up and swiftly drags the boxes inside. He then opens one. He finds some money and starts counting it.*

QUINN: Oh right! Looky looky. I'm rich!

(*pause*)

If I ruled the world, my cute face would 100% be on this bill.

NIC: U don't think the country would get fucked up?

QUINN: Naw man, the interest rate would go up.

NIC: Oh my God…U talkin' real comfortable for someone tellin' the wrong shit to his chick 'n getting' me in trouble, Mr Romeo. Opps are after me and keep getting 'the food'. Have you been talkin' about our business to your lady, little man?

NIC *pushes* QUINN *off the sofa, jokingly.*

QUINN: I'm not five. I dunno what you are askin' about.

NIC *chuckles and sits in an intimidating manner next to* QUINN. *He throws the box on the floor to make some space.*

NIC: (*inquisitive*) So, you did leave Leah, yeh?

QUINN: Yeh.

NIC: So, you ain't seeing her anymore, huh?

QUINN: Naw.

NIC: And you never told her shit about deliveries or anything?

QUINN: She's with Bladez now.

NIC: Hmm.

QUINN: Man, his pain runs deep.

NIC: What's there to be in pain about when you the king of the hood and you mekin' money without havin' to work. I wanna be like him.

QUINN: What?! Be part of a gang? You're crazy man. He now has more pain to give and he's gonna share it wiv the world. Jail never broke him and so he's come out tougher than when he first went inside. He's murderin' half the area and he's your boy?

(*confrontational*) Where's your chick, huh? Don't see you with any lady.

NIC *gives* QUINN *a stare.*

QUINN *backs away immediately, scared. He clings onto a pillow.*

NIC: Once u in war, it never endz. And he fucked someone as fine as your Leah? My type of man.

NIC *chuckles.*

HAMLIN *enters.*

HAMLIN: U lot tryna steal my socks or what?

NIC *playfully takes the pillow off* QUINN *and hits him with it.*

NIC: Q seems to think I can't get chicks, just coz Bladez and his people are back on the streets.

HAMLIN: So, a man comes back from pen and he's 'rewarded' with sex, maybe with another guy's girl…

(*beat*)

Maybe I need to chuck my CV away.

QUINN: Oookeey.

HAMLIN: How u not know dese men don't get shook and go in protective custody? U so sure that savage beast is still in him?

NIC: Well, I know I ain't goin' to no jail and I ain't dyin' a poor man either.

(*beat*)

Dem peoples say I can't be part of da fun. But am gonna show dem the Nic power! After Alex, I need a pack now! Who's with the lone wolf?

HAMLIN *and* QUINN *look at each other.*

NIC: I see ha…

(*sarcastic*) Still no job ha?

HAMLIN *tenses.*

NIC *smiles.*

NIC: So maybe you should listen.

(*pause*)

Ladies and gents, dogs and fart faces. I gotta solution for you.

NIC *brings a couple of the handbags out of a box.*

HAMLIN: (*whispers*) "Deliveries" here!? For Fu—

NIC: What u think of these?

NIC *snaps at* QUINN *to present the merchandise.* QUINN *obeys and wears one for show and tell.*

QUINN: Right, you can have this in blue, in red, they come in all sizes. Many pockets—

QUINN *attempts to open a zip but it's stuck.*

NIC: (*quickly gets the bag back*) Nah, give it back.

NIC *raises two similar looking handbags.*

NIC: Guess the difference?

QUINN *and* HAMLIN *just stare.*

NIC: Yep! This is one-fifty in a shop. I'll sell these fake ones on the high street for fifty quid instead.

HAMLIN: No deliveries to my mum's address, please!

QUINN: Nic, how u get hold of them?

NIC: From fam to fam. One word: Guildford. I give my contact money and he sends his friend to bring the package to me wherever I say. And then, I bring them here for safekeeping, in Hamlin's little nursery.

HAMLIN: Bro, come on. Please. Not here.

HAMLIN *frantically shoves the bags back in the box.*

HAMLIN: We'll become targets with dis shit here.

NIC: U pick and choose when you wanna puff ur chest, ha Ham?

(*pause*)

Why don't u grow sum balls and do it with me? Time u spend roamin' the streetz lookin' for a job. You wannabee stackin' shelves in sum shop like sum 9 to 5 civ? Believe me, this shit is easy. Listen to the teacher.

QUINN: I'm in!

NIC: What do you mean you are in? (*sighs*) I thought you were already?

QUINN: (*giggles*) Ham, come on, you could finally get a lady friend and she would be like "Oh Ham I need you in my life."

QUINN *chuckles.*

HAMLIN *gives him a stare.*

NIC *turns to* HAMLIN *inquisitively.*

NIC: U been laid yet?

QUINN *jokingly puts his arm around* HAMLIN.

HAMLIN *looks at both, annoyed, making sure* MAMA H. *is not in sight.*

NIC: Have you?

(*pause*)

Right… I don't need no bagz to get me a woman, but I sure need a fuckin' partner who can read a watch!

I was up at 5am waitin' for the delivery guy... waiting for 45 mins and someone decided not to show up on time!

(*to QUINN*) You ain't nothing like Alex waz...

QUINN: Uhm, I forgot I had to take my mum to the doctors.

NIC: (*mimicking*) "I forgot I had to take my mum to the doctors..." Are u sure u weren't doing something stupid? I waz so bored I even counted the fuckin' stars when they were out. Looked at the moon, missed it and almost cried. Hell, even the stars looked at me like I was a piece of shit. I thought, if I'm gonna make it big one day. I need those stars to line up like soldiers and agree!

QUINN: So, you finally started your own army of soldiers? I dun see anyone though.

NIC *stares at* QUINN.

NIC: As a man. U gotta fight sometimes. I guess ur dad never taught u that.

(*pause*)

I say two businesses at the same time. Two products. We sell the sniff and and we sell the bagz in Guildford.

QUINN *excitedly nods in agreement and puts his hoodie on.*

NIC: Guys, it is a goldmine out there, a goldmine. Forget that dumb job you were going for. We make our own new enterprise in this shit town. Fuck everybody. We are the new soldiers.

(*fist bumping all*)

It's Me—You—Quinn.

QUINN: Yeh. I've heard that dose rich kids there, when dey turn seventeen, they get a car. My Christmas vacations are going to Grandma's house across the street.

(*chuckles*)

HAMLIN: Yeh man, I feel dat. Dey havin' a shiny white Christmas while here we're starvin'.

QUINN: Exactly.

HAMLIN: (*lowers voice*) Alright, alright. Maybe I'll join in. Maybe.

(*beat*)

Juss promise me u not gonna bring your stuff here.

MAMA H. *calls* HAMLIN *from offstage*.

MAMA H: Hamlin?!

HAMLIN: (*whispering*) Catch you guys later. Take these boxes away please.

QUINN *and* NIC *gather everything*.

NIC: Think about it, Ham. Looks like ur mum needs sum help.

NIC *and* QUINN *grab the boxes and exit*.

HAMLIN *watches them leave, torn. From the other room he hears* MAMA H.

MAMA H: Oh my heart… Another boy found in the river, Hamlin!

HAMLIN *sits on the sofa, pensive.*

SCENE 7

Two months later. Afternoon. HAMLIN *is asleep on the sofa, again. He hears the doorbell and startles. Then peaks through the door.*

HAMLIN: Q? Dat you?!

QUINN: Pizza delivery!

HAMLIN: (*relaxed*): Is that a Sloppy G's with dough balls?

QUINN: At your service, big bro!

HAMLIN: With garlic bread?

QUINN: Come on man, open the door.

HAMLIN *opens the door and* QUINN *enters holding a pizza delivery box.*

HAMLIN: Not my fav, bro. That's your usual movie night F-up order! Dad used to have to eat it all cause we hated it.

HAMLIN *opens the box. Inside are a school notebook and a very old laptop.*

HAMLIN: What? Where did you get dis from?

QUINN: School. Dun tell anybody though.

HAMLIN: Thanks bro.

HAMLIN *notices* QUINN*'s new clothes.*

QUINN *turns like a fashion model showing off his new hoodie and trousers.*

HAMLIN *giggles but looks somewhat jealous.*

HAMLIN: Lookin' kinda fresh with ur new garms. And I get no love?

QUINN: I got love. I'm givin' the love back to my big bro. Look in the notebook. Gotta make sure you study while the "MAAN" here goes and hunts!

QUINN *beats his chest.*

QUINN: But also, finish your A levels and then promise you come with me, fam. It's the smarter choice.   ·

HAMLIN *finds 50 pounds in the notebook.*

HAMLIN: Wow...

QUINN: Born a sinner, now a winner. This is for havin' my back all dem times when u gave me the shirt off yours.

HAMLIN: So now u finally paying me in paper, yeh?

QUINN: Uh yeh.

HAMLIN: No more carrier bags full of pennies, yeh?

QUINN: Nah. I'm stackin' up now yeh. The Nic and Quinn duo. It's really happening man. Two successful months.

(*pause*)

You never show up.

HAMLIN: SHHH! I gotta a whole mum up in the house? U high?

QUINN: So, why your phone always off?

There is a buzz at the door. HAMLIN *freezes and checks the window.*

MAMA H: (*offstage*) Hamlin?

HAMLIN: (*to offstage*) It's just a delivery guy for next door, Mum!

(*pause*)

Man, these buzzers go off almost every day now. Freaks me out. We keep gettin' these warnings. The guy across from us went to prison 'cause he could not pay.

QUINN: Relax, bro, was juss a delivery.

HAMLIN: But what if dis house gets red-listed?

(*beat*)

Anyhow, how was Guildford?

QUINN: Guildford's got lots of green grass.

(*pause*)

I keep tellin' you. Come do this wiv me, H. I waz on the streetz and knew nothin' would happen to me out there.

HAMLIN: You sold the sniff too?

QUINN: I did

(*pause*)

But then I sold sum of that here too. And here, if you put ur guard down, u might actually die. Maybe I'm too soft for these streets. Not cut out for dis stuff here.

HAMLIN: Here? Not your territory, bro! Dis hood dun know you.

QUINN: And that's why every muscle from my toes, in my ass, to my dick started to pray. But I make a quick buck fam, den I mek it to ur house and I'm safe.

HAMLIN: What do u mean? You makin' this house an easy target!

QUINN: By the way, I'm not sure what stuff Leah told Bladez. She might have opened her mouth 'bout the bagz with Nic…

HAMLIN: So, you are still seeing her?! U never told her shit did u? Man, if Nic finds out.

QUINN: I like her. She understands me.

HAMLIN: And I don't? (*hurt*) Why you tryna be like Nic anyway?

QUINN: U want me to be broke like—

HAMLIN: Like me.

QUINN: Nah I juss wanna be invincible like him. So nobody can hurt me.

HAMLIN: You're losing it.

QUINN: I wish you would feed ur family for real and stop bein' legit. If u get caught doing sum dumb job, the endz are gonna laugh. U need to be stackin' coins.

HAMLIN: You know what I wish? I juss wish I could disappear.

QUINN: I wish I could disappear too. But I'm stuck in this life. I need to eat. I get sum cash in my hand and it's just stuck to my fist.

(*pause*)

Am thinkin' of dropping school too...

HAMLIN: Quinn—

QUINN: Am not a smart ass like you but am the one wearing new clothes.

(*pause*)

I need it, fam... Even though I have dreams that someone slashes me, like my spirit comes out my body—

HAMLIN: U sure the guy weren't me? Not like I'm tryna kill my friend but...

(*pause*)

Who to say I won't catch a body one day if I need to.

QUINN: Ham stop scarin' me, bro.

HAMLIN: I'm not scarin' shit. Look at you. You juss disappear. Dun even know you anymore.

(*beat*)

Ya know Nic didn't shed a tear at Alex's funeral?

(*beat*)

QUINN: Are you pissed cause I hang out with Nic?

HAMLIN: What?!

(*beat*)

You and Nic are delusional.

QUINN: No, you are!

HAMLIN: Whatever Q.

QUINN: Oh, F you Ham. I'm a yout still, but at least I got the nuts to mek bread for my family. What bout you?!

QUINN *puts on his hoodie and exits.*

HAMLIN *stands there, provoked.*

SCENE 8

Some days later. Early evening. HAMLIN *is in his house standing near the drying sage leaves. He breathes in and out, almost wanting to steal their energy.*

QUINN *and* NIC *are in front of* HAMLIN*'s house with beers, fancy clothes and shiny new phones.* NIC *rolls a blunt while* QUINN *dances to the beats, with his cap on backwards, speaking into his phone.*

QUINN: Get your bag up fellaz. This year it's all about chasin' the bag. Be leader. (*framing* NIC) Look at my bad ass friend.

NIC *kicks* QUINN *away.*

QUINN: Oook. Well peeps, be a—

HAMLIN: (*from the house*) Quinn, shut up.

QUINN: ...a man, a present to your girl and—

48

Annoyed, HAMLIN *storms out in his cheap clothes, leaving the door open behind him.*

HAMLIN: Quinn, I said shut up man!

HAMLIN *grabs* QUINN*'s phone and flicks the hat off* QUINN*'s head.*

QUINN: (*grabbing phone back*) Bro…

NIC *chuckles.*

HAMLIN: (*to* NIC) What you lot doing here? Am tryna study, so go sell your crap somewhere else.

While backing away HAMLIN *bumps into* NIC *making his cigarette fall on the floor. He then accidentally steps on it.*

NIC *gets up, confrontational.*

HAMLIN *shrinks.*

HAMLIN: Oh s-shit, I'm so sorry I-I…

QUINN *quickly places himself in the middle.*

QUINN: Ok, Ok. Juss chill man.

HAMLIN: It's cool Q, I don't need your help.

QUINN: What? (*to* NIC) Nic, my man, my bro. Calm it.

HAMLIN *takes the "bro" in.*

HAMLIN: (*to* QUINN) I said, I don't need your help Q!

Startled, QUINN *places his hat on* HAMLIN*'s head to break the ice.*

QUINN: Wait, uhm… King Hamlin… ha! Get it?

HAMLIN *struggles to smile.*

49

NIC *goes to roll another blunt.*

HAMLIN: I ain't no King. I fucked up. No job.

HAMLIN *throws the hat on the floor.*

QUINN: Ooookay.

(*annoyed*) Ham, you never show up. I told ya. Today's money problems could be solved. Tell him, Nic. (*whispers to* HAMLIN) Ham, I can top up ur phone, bro.

NIC: U ain't got no phone credit Ham? (*laughs*) Naw man. You wouldn't last a day in my shoes. (*looking down on* QUINN) You both, actually... I tell you dat no one gonna step to me no more now dat I am like a boss man. No more problems for Nic big man. Been thru more shit than you weak lot! Remember my dad even kickin' me out da house when I finally hit him back? I became a transformer that day.

NIC *flexes his muscles.*

QUINN: Yeah, you tell him, Nic. You juss have to be more like Nic. (*chuckles*) Then am sure you could help ur mum.

HAMLIN: (*sarcastic*) Be like Nic, yeh? Man-like-Nic.

NIC: Dat's right. Crackheads even got more hustle than you. Stop being a top dickhead and come to Guildford. Follow your big bro.

NIC *accidently knocks a pot of sage on the floor.*

HAMLIN *rushes to put it back in place.*

50

HAMLIN: Nic! Careful man! That's my mum's sage! It takes ages to grow. They supposed to bring this house luck.

NIC: Sorry

(*beat*)

Is it working though? Maybe I should put one in my pocket and then I'll be ok. Or maybe I juss...

NIC *stubs out some ash in the sage pot. Then he violently snips some leaves off and rolls another blunt with them.*

NIC: There, I feel safe already.

NIC *pretends to breath in and out his smoke on* HAMLIN'*s face.*

QUINN *instinctively laughs out loud. This hurts and gets on* HAMLIN'*s nerves.*

HAMLIN: You... You both with your... your fancy garms... and your fucking phones... and—

HAMLIN *suddenly grabs* QUINN'*s phone again and this time throws it on the floor. It cracks. He gasps. He can't believe he just did that.*

QUINN: Bro what's wrong wiv you?! That was new!

The boys look at each other in a moment of cold silence.

The sound of the electricity alarm key starts to beep very loudly.

51

NIC: So, what's it gonna be lil dickhead? You gonna roll with us now?

HAMLIN *surrenders.*

Lights out.

SCENE 9

Evening.

HAMLIN *is alone in the living room. He looks at his reflection in the mirror, topless. With no electricity, there is just a little flashlight on the table.*

HAMLIN: I ain't no dickhead, you know! (*screaming to self*) Now stop bein' a dickhead!? Why you let peoples treat you like that? What, you ain't a man? What, Q am not your bro anymore? Huh? Nic better huh? (*his voice raises*) Why you let people go walking all over you? Why you take dat— it's funny? You wanna stand there and laugh at me? Why you laughin' at me! You wanna slap me in my face? Which one of you lot wants it! What?! W-what?!...Hold me back! Hold me back. Don't make me fight! The streetz are callin', the bills are callin'. Gonna be like Nic. Naw, you know what?! Better than him.

HAMLIN *is out of breath, staring in the mirror.*

HAMLIN: Nic.

(*pause*)

HAMLIN: Why you whistling so loudly, bro? Anywayz, Nic, I'm coming dis time. You better be right.

HAMLIN *quickly looks for his hat. He poses in front of the mirror and tries to pump his chest.*

Lights out.

INTERVAL

SCENE 10

Night.

HAMLIN and QUINN are in a derelict area waiting for NIC.

QUINN is fiddling with sage leaves in his pocket.

They stand there in silence, distant from each other.

QUINN: Remember me and you playin' in the sandpit?

(*pause*)

You'd be walkin' and I'd be behind puttin' my feet in your footprints.

HAMLIN doesn't reply.

Even back then I thought: I wanna be like him.

HAMLIN gives him a stare. QUINN attempts to connect once more.

QUINN: If I had your head—

HAMLIN: You don't tho.

QUINN: Right.

(*pause*)

You're way ahead.

HAMLIN doesn't reply.

QUINN: Come on Ham… So what now. I'm dumb and don't deserve my shit?

HAMLIN: Yes.

QUINN: Why? You're here too now.

(*beat*)

Lettin' my new drip come tween us?

HAMLIN: I read dat slaves from the master's plantation used to fight amongst each other over which slave master was wealthier or had the nicest stuff.

(*pause*)

I guess nothing's changed.

The sound of NIC *whistling 'Baa baa black sheep' is heard, but he is nowhere to be seen.*

Then, a light from a lamppost shines on NIC *as he approaches the boys, amusing himself for his grand entrance.*

NIC: My boyz.

As if jealous, NIC *walks in between the boys to separate them and to attract more attention for himself.*

NIC: I woulda sworn I was in Guildford 10 min ago. I take a walk and I'm here. Funny dat.

QUINN: Hey—

HAMLIN *and* QUINN *notice something odd on* NIC*'s face. He has a fresh scar on a cheek.*

NIC: See, Hamlin has finally grown some balls. Welcome, my little pet.

NIC *pats* HAMLIN *on the head.* HAMLIN *says nothing.*

NIC: (*standing on a bench*) Now, are you manz ready to ride out? Are you lot ready for war?!

QUINN *pats his chest repeatedly.*

QUINN: Yeah! Yes, I am.

NIC: (*to* QUINN) Now Q!

Distracted, QUINN *is turned the other way.*

QUINN: Huh? Huh what?

NIC: Q! Over here.

QUINN: Yo! What?

NIC: Q, I hope your bitch was right about this place. (*to* HAMLIN) Hamlin, come here for a minute. Something serious.

(*beat*)

You forgot to put on your leash.

NIC *laughs as he jokingly shoves* HAMLIN *away.*

NIC: Now, I will show them who the new king is with dis.

NIC *takes a knife out of his pocket, dangling it with pride.*

QUINN *is visibly uncomfortable.*

HAMLIN *gives him a stare.*

The boys start to overlap each other when talking.

HAMLIN: (*to* QUINN) What the fuck man!

HAMLIN *starts leaving.*

NIC: (*to* HAMLIN) Don't you dare chicken out on me now!

QUINN: (*to both*) I thought we... I thought we were just gonna sell sum stashes.

(*pause*)

I... I don't know bout dis Nic.

HAMLIN: (*to* QUINN) I'm done with you.

NIC*'s nerves are hit. He points the machete at* QUINN.

NIC: Stop being a pathetic loser, you little bitch. You are the worst business partner ever.

QUINN *is hurt.*

NIC *points the knife at* QUINN *and* HAMLIN.

HAMLIN: Nic, Put that ting down.

NIC *points the knife now at* HAMLIN.

QUINN: What's wrong with you?!

NIC: Relax guys. Juss playn' innit.

(*puts knife down*)

You know, dem people on the corner tonight are just a bunch of kids lookin' for about six points.

HAMLIN: Points?

NIC: We gonna get em to back off from our corners. Cause I decided they are now ours. Someone stole our deliveries yesterday cause Q is too dumb to even remember to collect dem. Those fuck heads had all da time to snatch our stuff.

QUINN: I thought you said the delivery was tomorrow!

HAMLIN: Dis is not what you s-said over the phone. I don't—

NIC: (*flicks HAMLIN's hat off*)

Look at my face yeh? Am I a wimp? Gotta give dis (*points to scar*) some meaning.

HAMLIN *grabs his hat back.*

NIC *looks excited.*

NIC: Dis is an new adventure guys! What u lot so serious for? Ha? I see a funeral. I see da flowers. And then I see a family. Dey gotta cry them tears! Too much fun.

HAMLIN: You proper losing it?

NIC: OMG, I'm playin'.

HAMLIN: What if someone sees us! What-what about the police?

NIC: They fightin' the same villains we fighting, but they think we're the villains. Hamlin, they don't care about us.

NIC *laughs and hands* QUINN *the knife.*

NIC: TAKE the knife!

QUINN *grabs the knife, hesitantly and nervously.*

NIC: Hero of the day.

QUINN *stares at the knife and looks at* HAMLIN *for an approval which he does not get.*

NIC: Wipe that milk off your mouth, Quinn. Show me you are a man.

QUINN: We da only ones who ever follow you and your fake army. How we not know you ain't all BS?

QUINN *puts the knife down.*

NIC: U ain't no warrior.

HAMLIN *sees something from afar.*

HAMLIN: Guys? Ain't dat Bladez's mandem by dat bus stop?

NIC: Yas! (*excited*) We gonna come to that pathway. When I say "go", we gonna cut and round em up.

(*pause*)

Go go go go! They are leaving!

NIC *puts his hoodie on and runs towards the bus stop. A faint police siren is heard in the background.* HAMLIN *and* QUINN *halt.*

NIC: Hamlin, come on! Q, move your ass!

The sound of the bus moving away is heard. Terrified, HAMLIN *and* QUINN *start leaving, chickening out.*

NIC: Oh man, you pieces of shit! Why you slown' me down?!

QUINN: What's dis tryna be a big man, ha? Whatever red U got flowin' through you, I ain't got it. Game over. I'm going home.

NIC: (*pointing the knife*) No backbone. Dis mess
is your fault and you can't even be a real
man about it. Bladez knows our every move
because of you and your big mouth snitch
bitch. You ruin my war.

HAMLIN: (*scared*) Nic, put that ting down.
Please… please!

NIC: You lot ain't for da streetz. (*to* QUINN)
Betcha that Leah of yours has her dayz
counted. The young Romeo my ass—

QUINN *charges at* NIC. *They struggle.*

HAMLIN *steps forwards trying to separate
the two boys which leads to* NIC
accidentally stabbing QUINN.

QUINN *fatally falls to the ground.*

*There is a moment of petrified realization of
what just happened.*

HAMLIN: (*rushing to* QUINN) Quinn!

NIC *stays there frozen unable to accept
what he just did. He drops the knife.*

*Another police siren is heard in the
background.*

NIC *impulsively picks the knife. He grabs*
HAMLIN*'s arm to pull him away.*

HAMLIN *looks at* QUINN *one last time and
reluctantly exits.*

Lights out.

SCENE 11

The morning after. NIC *has a movie on his phone in* HAMLIN*'s living room while he looks for food on the kitchen shelves.*

HAMLIN *sits on the sofa, frozen. He clutches at a sage branch and at a pillow.*

NIC: I swear the only thing I can make in dis house is a sardine sandwich. No thanks.

   NIC *looks at* HAMLIN, *has a moment, then continues as if it were nothing.*

NIC: Anyhow… ordered sum Chinese for us.

   HAMLIN *does not reply.*

NIC: You think I'm not gonna hook up my soldier and keep him fed?

   (*pause*)

   Yeh coz that's what a boss does.

   (*pause*)

   Yeh man.

   NIC *sits and pulls out some money.*

NIC: Anything you need, bills made. I got you, man. You're my friend.

   HAMLIN *does not reply.*

   NIC *starts watching the film.*

NIC: That's right Michael B. Jordan! You tell em!

   NIC *peaks* HAMLIN*'s way but gets no reaction.*

61

NIC: Look, am only tryna be helpful. Don't cook well like your mum. Don't worry, Ham. I got some extra for Mum for when she's home.

(*beat*)

That's my man Michael! The dude chose not to go with his slave masters. Instead, he drops in the ocean to be with his ancestors, 'coz he said death is better than bondage. Now that's deep.

NIC *pretends to play fist fight. He hits* HAMLIN*'s on the head jokingly.*

HAMLIN *does not react.*

NIC: Oh com on, Ham.

(*pause*)

Q was still seeing dat chick 'coz Bladez wasn't lookin' too happy des days. Snitch. Totally unreliable. He fucked up real bad.

HAMLIN *clings onto more sage leaves.* NIC *is lost for more words and looks the other way.*

NIC: His boyz are everywhere, stealin' all our stuff. They are leavin' nothing for us. Now they're even selling stashes in Guildford.

(*long pause*)

Quinn's stinky mouth even snitched something about our goldmine. (unsure) Am, am sure he did… He did yes…

HAMLIN *brings the leaves to his nose and starts breathing them in.*

NIC *takes the sage out of* HAMLIN*'s hands.*

NIC: That shit don't work.

HAMLIN *violently grabs the sage back and pushes* NIC *out of the way*.

NIC *looks surprised, yet satisfied*.

NIC: Q had it in his pocket, um um… yeh, yeh, that's right, Q asked for it by havin' it in his pocket and look where he is now. In some street corner, if they ain't found him already.

HAMLIN: We could have saved him. I could have—

NIC: Toughen up, Ham—

HAMLIN: Are you mad, fam?

NIC: He was never gonna make it. It's his fault. Yes, yes…

(*pause*)

I only helped him leave sooner before someone else got him.

(*beat*)

In fact, in a way, Bladez street boys are to blame.

HAMLIN *turns to stare at* NIC.

HAMLIN: What!?

NIC: Yes, yes, they are to blame! They should pay for what they did.

HAMLIN *is in disbelief*.

NIC: Fuck them!

(*beat*)

Time to step up now, Hamlin. You a soldier now. Be like ME.

HAMLIN: No thank you.

NIC: (*offended*) Yaw know, I've seen the white meat. I've seen cuts all the way to the bones. The scars stay for the rest of your life. I ain't afraid of them. No sir. Alex, I was there when dey fighting. He became a beast after he got cut and went out lookin' to stab the next madem. A real man.

(*pause*)

You gotta fight back dese days. No time for cryin'.

HAMLIN *turns the other way. This motivates* NIC *to speak more convincingly. He lifts his jumper. Three old knife wound scars are visible on his chest.*

NIC: A real man, yes...

(*pause*)

U know when a man's skin is open and that shit is the perfect line, a perfect scar. The first time, Doctor told me dey got me an inch away from my heart.

(*pause*)

It happened fast. The second time I got cut, in seconds I went from hyper-dude to stabbed. Went into a foetal position on the floor gaspin' for air. Survival kicked in—so I'm thinkin' "I wanna rip your head off, I wanna need kill you."

HAMLIN *just stares.*

NIC: I'ma let them know my name is my name.
That's how you pump your chest like a man.
If you can't box, you gotta slice a man.
(unsure) You gotta... If you don't, you're just
as good as dead.

(pause)

Dead like Quinn...

NIC *is affected by his words but fumbles his
way out to hide it. He continues on his self-
preach.*

NIC: What's the difference between sum posh
twat sayin' "Give me liberty or give me
death" or me walkin' around sayin' "I don't
give a fuck?"

HAMLIN: He was my bro... *(holds tears back)*
I'll tell everybody what you did.

NIC: I did?

(pause)

I did nothin'. *(grins)* Or maybe you did? Who
do you think they're gonna believe? A white
boy or a black boy?

(pause)

Don't you dare. This is between you and me
only!

NIC *points an intimidating finger at*
HAMLIN.

HAMLIN *suddenly looks concerned and
scared.*

NIC: I'm sick of people fucking with me! I am
da new boss! Won't let anyone say I no good

for the hood. You and your pissy mattress. Hell, you think you can juss be out when you want? You are in dis as much as I am. You were there. Savages can smell the fear and they devour. They leave you smellin', rotting, like Quinn's body YOU left behind.

(*pause*)

I say it's hunting season!

HAMLIN *looks at* NIC.

NIC: What?! What are you lookin' at? Do you think I deserved to die instead of Q? Do I look like a monster? Am I a monster?

NIC *is fully energized and out of his mind.*

HAMLIN *looks at him not entirely sure if he is joking or not.*

NIC: I said, will you fuck society with me or not?!! Will you take from Bladez what he took from Quinn? Do you wanna take down those dicks who killed your dad?

(*pause*)

I'm the new Bladez! This is good dirt standin' right here. Nic is good dirt, good seed standin' right here dis second! So, you with me or not!? I'm society's child! I'm society's fucking child! This is how they made me!

(*pause*)

I gotta World War Three comin'! There will be a new king! Believe! (*beats his chest*) Hamlin, you roll with me now.

NIC *places his hand on* HAMLIN*'s shoulder.*
HAMLIN *stands there frozen and scared,*
reluctantly brainwashed.

SCENE 12

The same day. Afternoon.

HAMLIN *walks down a street coming back*
from school. He is on duty selling stashes
looking around as if waiting for someone to
come buy a stash. For a moment, he thinks he
sees QUINN.

HAMLIN: Quinn?! (*unsure*) Yo Quinn, wait for
me. I'm sorry—I'm—

The boy turns around to reveal he is not
QUINN. *He moves closer in an intimidating*
manner.

Suddenly a punch out of nowhere is swung
in HAMLIN*'s stomach.*

HAMLIN: What the—

HAMLIN *is strong enough to block the*
person and they struggle for a while. His
school bag and stashes are ripped off him.

HAMLIN: No!

HAMLIN *places his hands in his pockets and*
realizes that there is nothing in there
anymore.

HAMLIN: No, no no…NO-NO. Fuck!!!! I thought
I saw your face. I'm sick of all this man!
What did I tell you?! I told you not to do

thissss! Stupid Q. U didn't listen. I ain't goin' down like you. Not in the ground.

Transition lights. Evening.

HAMLIN *walks home and goes to his room, ignoring* MAMA H. *He comes back in wearing a hoodie, feeling different and walking with an attitude.*

MAMA H: Hamlin?

MAMA H. *stares at him for a moment, swiftly removes his hoodie. She then goes to her sage plants, disappointed. Trying to breathe in and out and stay calm.*

Feeling uncomfortable, HAMLIN *picks up a bin bag, sees the transformer toy on the table, has a moment, but then bins it. He starts making his way outside.*

MAMA H: If I'ma leave this Earth one day, I wanna trust you can take care of yourself coz the system won't. Juss like they ain't helping me, us.

HAMLIN: We both know I'm likely to be gone first.

(*pause*)

I'll tell Dad that you said hi…

MAMA H: Stop it. Don't do this to me Hamlin. Your mum ain't stupid.

HAMLIN: Yeh. I know u ain't.

MAMA H: Why u breathin' heavy at night?

HAMLIN: Whys I keep breathin'...

MAMA H: I hear u.

HAMLIN: I... I keep having these dreams.

MAMA H: What dreams?

HAMLIN: Dreamin' I'm... laying in my bed and I keep hearing these footsteps and they keep coming closer and closer and closer and... I don't know whether I'm dreamin' or whether it's real... every night they just keep comin' closer.

(*pause*)

MAMA H: U keep listenin' closer for them footsteps. That's Dad watching over you.

HAMLIN: He used to say if anything happened to him, he'd fight for me in Heaven so that I could live.

MAMA H: And he is. He fought for u.

HAMLIN: All I see around me is hate. When I walk down the streets the next thing I know, I'm in another hood and I feel I'm huntin'. Fight breaks out in no time.

(*pause*)

My first thinkin' is, I wanna attack to defend myself.

(*pause*)

It meks me scared of what I wanna do... I feel this new energy, like, like I'm another person. Like I want to learn to be a hero.

MAMA H. *looks concerned.*

HAMLIN: Everyone in the world hates boys that look like me, Mum. Brown boys.

(*long beat*)

MAMA H: You mean like Quinn?

HAMLIN: Huh??

MAMA H: Where is he?

HAMLIN: He uh…

MAMA H: Hamlin?

HAMLIN: What?

MAMA H: My baby Quinn sage plant is all dry… not cause of me, dis time. Hamlin? Is he okay? His mother called me as he never went home. Hope he ain't gettin' involved in sum street stuff. Don't lie.

(*long beat*)

HAMLIN: He's cool. Maybe he went to his girl.

MAMA H: (*suspicious*) I need u boyz lookin' out for each other. Stay out of trouble.

(*beat*)

Promise me you are gonna walk tall like your father, like the Hamlin King you are.

HAMLIN: (*hesitant*) I promise.

(*beat*)

MAMA H: Let me show u somethin'.

MAMA H. *takes* HAMLIN *outside to show him a skinny bloomed sage.*

HAMLIN *places the bin bag down.*

MAMA H: Look at her. Not a bad look for such a rocky root. I needed you to see the seed grow in the dirty soil. I wanted you to be proud. Nan would be proud…

(*pause*)

Ain't she beautiful? My beautiful Hamlin.

(*pause*)

I love you.

MAMA H. *looks at* HAMLIN *concerned, then enters the house.*

Pensive, HAMLIN *puts his hoodie back on and then goes back inside.*

Transition lights.

NIC *enters. He turns around to check nobody is looking and puts a coin into the electric meter. The garden lights come on. He then takes a new fully-grown sage plant out of his bag and places it near the front door. A tag on it reads "Nic".*

SCENE 13

The next day.

NIC *is in a park waiting for* HAMLIN.

HAMLIN *enters wearing his baggy old trousers, his new hoodie, and a cap placed backwards.*

NIC *laughs.*

HAMLIN: What's so funny ?

NIC: (*fixes* HAMLIN*'s hat*) You. You look dressed like a cartoon version of Quinn... only you're no snake. Am I right, huh? You've been a good boy for three days... now don't go being stupid.

NIC *places his fingers on* HAMLIN*'s lips as if to shush him, then points a finger at him.*

HAMLIN *suddenly feels uncomfortable.*

NIC: Now. Ham. Hello?

HAMLIN *looks away.*

NIC: Come on. Snap out of it, Ham! Right, lesson number one. Let's play the scoreboard.

HAMLIN: The what?

NIC: It takes a real man to throw a few swings. Show me what you've got.

NIC *squares off in a boxing position.*

HAMLIN *tries to follow, but he just can't snap out of his depression.*

NIC: Okay so Ham, put ur fist up yeh... right... Now Hamlin yeh. You could be walkin' down the South endz and sum dude comes up to you yeh—he's not gonna stop you and say, "sorry bro, are you part of the dis crew?" If he don't know you, he's just gonna stab you... Where u think he's aiming?

HAMLIN: The heart.

NIC Naw. It's da head first. It's 50 points for the head. Da highest score. The heart is only 30 points.

NIC *jabs for* HAMLIN*'s head.* HAMLIN *tries to block this but is unsuccessful.*

Man-up Hamlin!

HAMLIN: What?!

NIC: Block me!

(*beat*)

Look bro, I'm tryin' to look after you, yeh, I am tryin' to protect you, us. So, wek up, yeah?

HAMLIN: (*reluctantly*) Well, if he tries to steal from me—

NIC: He ain't gonna be stealin' from u, just gonna stab you!!

HAMLIN: Yeh, I know—

NIC: He's gonna shank you. Right here.

NIC *pretends to aim for* HAMLIN*'s heart* but HAMLIN *manages to block him this time. He looks revived and very pleased by this.*

NIC: Dat's could have been 30 points. Yeh? Ok, well done.

(*beat*)

Now, let's just say you get lucky and you about to do a runner, yeh?

NIC *and* HAMLIN *continue to square up.*

NIC: Now if I'm a little yout and I'm new and I gotta lil knife... I'm aimin' for your legs. Das a quick 10 points and a quick way to rise up the ranks.

HAMLIN: I ain't tryna be in no gang.

73

NIC: Remember what I said. You ain't got no choice. In dis hood, you're involved no matter what. Don't you be stupid.

HAMLIN *struggles to accept this.*

NIC: Now, you see dat knife slashing meat in the kebab shops over there yeh. Why you think they get stolen?

HAMLIN *turns around and, while distracted, NIC pretends to point to* HAMLIN*'s heart, holding the pose.*

NIC: Aaand my 30 points! If I get up the ranks, I become a leader—controlling 15-20 kids, tellin' them what to do.

HAMLIN: What is this point shit?

NIC *pretends to strike for* HAMLIN*'s head.*

HAMLIN *block him again and the feeling is great.*

NIC: This point shit popped up on my phone the other day. TikTok stuff. You would know if ya had a phone. So, do you wanna become a big man, a hunter?

HAMLIN: Ah man, ok ok!

NIC *sneaks another hit.*

NIC: Bam! Got you in the head! 50 points for me. Now I'm the leader.

HAMLIN *looks annoyed yet is finally convinced and smiles. The boys fistbump.*

SCENE 14

Later that day. Evening.

HAMLIN *enters.*

MAMA H. *stands outside her the door as if she has seen a ghost.*

HAMLIN *is startled and goes to her.*

HAMLIN: Mum! Mum what is it?

MAMA H. *can barely speak.*

MAMA H: My plant Hamlin... my plant has died.

HAMLIN: What... Mum?

MAMA H: Q's plant. I knew it... I knew it. His mum called.

HAMLIN *is suddenly silent.*

MAMA H: His mum said the last she saw him, he was fixing his school bag and then he was gone for many hours. He never went back home. Was two days ago.

HAMLIN: What?!

HAMLIN *turns away, unable to look* MAMA H. *in the eyes.*

(*beat*)

MAMA H: They found his body this morning. They have no clue who did it.

(*pause*)

The police be lookin' and they called here.

(*pause*)

MAMA H: Hamlin?

HAMLIN *looks stone dead.*

MAMA H: They want you to go in to chat to them?

(*pause*)

Don't be scared baby. You're not like des boys. They are juss hungry! Ain't no one paving the way. Their mothers raised them in abuse, and they want to ride around with the pain!

(*pause*)

And I can't help them no more.

(*pause*)

Hamlin?

MAMA H *reaches out for her son, but* HAMLIN *rejects her and impulsively exits.*

MAMA H: Hamlin!

MAMA H. *painfully enters the house.*

SCENE 15

Weeks later, evening.

HAMLIN e*nters in the dark, the electricity key beeps.* HAMLIN *puts in a coin.*

HAMLIN *is dressed in all black fashionable designer clothes. With baggy trousers and his hoodie, he now looks more confident and in control—a bad boy with a shiny new watch on his wrist and a new phone.*

MAMA H. *enters.*

HAMLIN: (*on the phone*) That was mad, fam, had mad love for dat still. Sorted it out, bro.

Yo, Mum, what you sayin'?

silence

MAMA. H: Yo M-u-m what you s-a-y-i-n'?

HAMLIN: Why u all dolled up for?

MAMA. H: Dolled up? For who? I'm tryna change job. The money is not enough. Am thinkin' Teacher Assistant or somethin'.

HAMLIN *is distracted.*

Hello?

HAMLIN: (*disinterested*) Oh yeh, congrats.

HAMLIN *messages on his phone.*

MAMA H: Hello?

HAMLIN: Ha? Oh sorry. Sum gyal posted something dumb on Insta. Gotto go soon.

MAMA H: Been few weeks now and every time I wake up you goin' out. Hamlin, you need to speak to someone maybe... I know you're hurtin... but keeping busy and talkin' like that isn't—

HAMLIN: Am busy mekin' sure you eat.

HAMLIN *makes his way.*

MAMA H. *looks at him displeased.*

MAMA H: They will never hire you lookin' like that!

HAMLIN *takes the comment in.*

MAMA H: What did your father tell you about dressin' like that? You look like a suspect.

HAMLIN: And now you mekin' me wanna leave when u say his name.

(*beat*)

Dis is my new drip. It's me now, innit. Don't need no interviews. Dey don't need me.

(*beat*)

Should I tek my clothes off and give em to you?

(*pause*)

I mean got no coins left but I got a few notes dat I could give u—

MAMA H: Hamlin?

HAMLIN: What, you want me naked?

MAMA H: I want you to act right and remember your father's layin' in the cemetery protectin' you.

HAMLIN: But he ain't here is he, huh? Stop checkin' on me. I don't need you.

This hurts

MAMA H: I know you're hurting. I know Q—

HAMLIN: No.

HAMLIN *accidently knocks a sage pot on the floor. He looks at the mess, horrified, but then—*

HAMLIN: It ain't workin' anyways. It's shit. It's a stupid old Nan shit.

Long cold silence, MAMA H. *is in shock.*

NIC*'s 'Baabaa black sheep' whistles are heard from outside.*

HAMLIN*'s phone buzzes. He gets money out his pocket, counts the notes and puts them on the table.*

HAMLIN: Rent.

(*pause*)

It's done. Make my own luck. I'm da man of this house now.

Speechless. MAMA H. *sits on the sofa.*

HAMLIN *exits.*

Lights up outside.

NIC *waits for* HAMLIN *near the usual hang out wall.*

NIC: Big props to u lil man, proud of u.

HAMLIN: Yo, fam, why the urgent call?

NIC: It's us or dem. They tryna do us. Manz tried to show me a machete and are selling all over Guilford. Now we gotta let those kids know who's ruling. Gonna score dem points.

HAMLIN: I thought this was a quick job ting. Dis sounds like sum other beef. You never say everything.

NIC: I need someone I can rely on. You can't be slippin' now.

HAMLIN: Nic man. I'm tired.

NIC: What?

HAMLIN: Been workin' my ass off for you. So, am FUCKIN' tired!

NIC *looks almost impressed by the attitude, but then hovers over* HAMLIN.

NIC: As I said, you too involved now. Dey know where you live and where we hang out. (*challenging*) Besides, I think dey the ones were involved when your father got shanked.

HAMLIN: (*takes a breath*) What?!

NIC: So, when u gonna get ur P's and get the respect u deserve if ur always bottom of the pile?

NIC *and* HAMLIN *put their hoodies on and exit.*

SCENE 16

Later that evening. A dim light peers through the living room window of HAMLIN*'s house.*

A man, dressed in a black hoodie, approaches. He starts vandalizing the front porch. He spreads all the bin bag rubbish and knocks the sage pots.

Lights rise on MAMA H. *as she stands in the middle of it all, speechless and about to break down.*

MAMA H. *kneels to pick up her broken pots.*

MAMA H: Naw, naw my babies. Not my babies…

(*beat*)

Nan, I'm sorry … fucked up… I fucked up…

A moment and MAMA H. *gets up decisively.*

MAMA H: We ain't doing this today, not in my house… not with my children. You youngens, all you see is demons!

MAMA H. *storms back in the house with her broken pots.*

Transition lights.

The boys are in an alleyway. There is a BOY *there with knife in hand, scared to use it.*

HAMLIN: Noooo! Noooooo!

The BOY *reaches for* HAMLIN*'s leg, hitting it.* HAMLIN *gives a piercing scream.* NIC *stands to the side, scared.*

NIC: Ham! Ham! Come on!

NIC slide his knife to HAMLIN. *It's too far from his reach.*

HAMLIN: I can't do it Nic, I can't do it!

NIC: Even Q laying in a pool of blood has not manned you up now! It's you or him.

THE BOY *reaches for* HAMLIN *again and hits him hard.* HAMLIN *falls on the floor.*

HAMLIN: Fuck you, dickhead!

NIC: Hamlin, watch out!

The BOY *swings a punch in* HAMLIN*'s stomach. Nearly there to deliver the final death sentence.*

Taken suddenly by a wave of anger, HAMLIN *flips the boy over, punching him endlessly.*

HAMLIN: You fuckin' piece of shit. YOU Fuckin'…

The rage is so overwhelming, even NIC cannot believe what he is seeing.

(*very long beat*)

HAMLIN *leans on top of the boy's body, panicked and in disbelief.*

NIC *slowly picks up the knife and places it back in his pocket.*

NIC: Thanks for havin' my back, bro.

HAMLIN: Oh, Shut up man! I never wanted this. Not this far.

NIC: Deep shit now for you, lil man. (*points at body on floor*) Ham, I've been stabbed, what? Three times now. Been crucified by the police. Pissed on from the hood. I'm walkin' around with the thorns on.

(*beat*)

And you? You were fresh meat out there. One of da real manz see you comin', you's finished. So, be proud today.

HAMLIN: I said shut up man! I ain't your bro no more. Look at what you made me do. (*breathing heavily*) What did I—

NIC: What I made you do?

(*pause*)

Don't go blamin' me for what you do. Cause of your fuck ups, people been pointin' at me. But now, I ain't protectin' you no more.

HAMLIN: Protect me! How?! You got me and Q into this shit!

NIC: I juss helped Q take the pain away.

HAMLIN: You're crazy!

HAMLIN *stands up aggressively keeping his hand on his aching leg.*

NIC *suddenly feels threatened.*

NIC: Don't look at me like I'm a loser.

(*beat*)

Yes, I am crazy, but you know what else? I don't give a shit.

(*pause*)

I don't give a shit about Q, I give a shit about you. I don't even give a shit about myself.

(*beat*)

Too bad what you did to Quinn and to that boy.

HAMLIN: What?!

NIC: Check out the halo on my head. (*beats chest*) 'King Nic.'

NIC *violently pushes* HAMLIN, *but* HAMLIN *pushes him back, squaring off to him.*

HAMLIN: What! Come on. Let's go then! Runnin' up your mouth, let's see!

NIC *swings a punch, but* HAMLIN *ducks quickly.*

HAMLIN: Is dis the best war you got?

NIC: (*scared*) Y-you're juss like your dead dad.

(*pause*)

You're juss like him.

NIC *swings another punch, but* HAMLIN *fends it off, then grabs* NIC *by the shirt.*

HAMLIN: Get out of here, before I fuck you up!

NIC: (*unsure*) You don't really have the balls.

NIC *desperately attempts to push* HAMLIN *again but* HAMLIN *blocks him.*

HAMLIN: You ain't no King... (*flips* NIC*'s hat off*)

You ain't shit.

NIC *is hurt and backs away scared.*

NIC: Am gonna let everyone know what YOU did!

You're a coward.

NIC *exits pointing the knife at* HAMLIN.

NIC: (*scared*) You juss like Q yeah, juss like Q…

NIC *dries his sudden tears.*

…you fuck me over man… it is over for you… (*desperate*) "slash"!

NIC *exits.*

HAMLIN *stands there confused between the new powerful energy he just found and the fear of death.*

HAMLIN: I'm tired of this shiiit!

HAMLIN *swings in the air.*

HAMLIN: I'm so fucking tired of this shit…

HAMLIN *swings again.*

Fuck this shit! Fuck you, motherfucker! Fuck you with this death shit! Come on den get me, come and get, I'm standing right here. I'll kill you. Come on death! Come on death! Bring my dad while you're at it as well.

(*beat*)

Where were you, where were you for my birthday, New Year, Christmas, when Mum was cryin' huh? Where were you? How am I gonna tell my kids dey got no grandad ha?

(*pause*)

Why u have to die like dat, tryna be da hero and that? But you ain't nothin' but a bitch. I'm the one tryna be a man now.

(*pause*)

I can't do this.

(*pause*)

Come and get me, Mr. Death. Yo, boss man. Mr. Death bring your crew, bring your gang and face me like a man. Juss tek my last breath and let me rest... please.

Sound of sirens. HAMLIN *leaves in a hurry with his aching leg.*

He drags himself home, stops just before the front door realizing what has been done to his house.

(beat)

HAMLIN *suddenly barges in the house going straight for the table. His walk is troubled.*

MAMA H. *notices and rushes towards him.*

(long beat)

MAMA H: Hamlin?

(*beat*)

Hamlin!

HAMLIN: I ain't got no time.

MAMA H: No. It's been weeks you acting weird.

HAMLIN *'s phone buzzes.* MAMA H. *grabs his phone and slams it on the table.*

MAMA H: Not this streets shit. Have you seen my front porch?

HAMLIN: Let me go!

MAMA H: NO. Listen to me.

(*beat*)

Sometimes I'm hurtin' thinkin' that your Dad's not alive. I'm sorry. And now Q. God, I'm sorry.

HAMLIN: Mama—

MAMA H: Sorry that... I didn't teach you how to fight. U have all these dreams. I mean this area has the Devil's children. A happy child won't have the heart to walk up to someone and cut them to pieces—

HAMLIN: Ma, let me go. None of your fu—

(*pause*)

It's not your business.

MAMA H: Lord knows you could be thinking about being sum lawyer, or a software engineer... but not with that mouth. I mean, I'm not perfect, but I don't wanna see my imperfect baby laying in his father's pool of blood.

(*this hits*)

When a mother hears her boy's been stabbed, she feels him kicking in her heart. And—it—hurts. Hamlin, it hurts me.

(*beat*)

I never asked you where the smart meter payments came from, all your new clothes, your phone… because I didn't want to hear you lie to me.

HAMLIN *doesn't reply.*

MAMA H: Never lie to me!

HAMLIN: Mum, I said none of your fucking business!

MAMA H. *slaps* HAMLIN *who stands there petrified.*

MAMA H: Don't you do that! Did I make things so bad? I'm supposed to die first. I'll leave you first!

HAMLIN *pulls himself together and starts looking through the mess of objects on the table.*

MAMA H: God dammit Hamlin! Hamlin?!

HAMLIN *finds gardening scissors.* MAMA H *gasps. It is not clear yet what Hamlin intends doing with it until he goes for the door.* MAMA H. *desperately follows him.*

MAMA H: Oh, so you tough and you wanna go out and hurt somebody? Go on, stab me then.

HAMLIN *does not turn around.*

MAMA H: What? You wanna end up like Alex in the cemetery… or Quinn on the side of a street?

HAMLIN *freezes.*

MAMA H: Don't you think I know.?

(*pause*)

MAMA H: What is a mother to think…

HAMLIN *doesn't reply.*

MAMA H: Give me the bloody scissors, Hamlin!

HAMLIN *finally exits.*

MAMMA H. *follows.*

HAMLIN: NIC! NIC! I know you're here hidin'. Dis ain't your home anymore! Come face me like a man! Come get ur fuckin' points!

HAMLIN *desperately swings the knife in air.*

NIC *is hiding in a corner crying, clinging on the sage plant with his name on it.*

QUINN*'s ghost sits on the garden low wall, watching him.*

HAMLIN: Where are you, you piece of shit! Hiding like a baby? Admit it bro, the only reason why you still standin' above ground is coz ur too much of a coward to take your own life.

(*pause*)

Look at me now. Do I look like monster yet? Do I?!

HAMLIN *lifts his hoodie to expose his clean chest.*

HAMLIN: This is good dirt standin' right here.

(*beats chest*)

Hamlin is good dirt. I'm society's child. I'm society's FUCKING CHILD! This is how YOU made me.

(*beat*)

89

HAMLIN: Check out the halo on MY head.

(*pause*)

King fuckin' Hamlin.

HAMLIN *beats his chest repeatedly.*

HAMLIN: He was my bro. How could you! How could I... I left you layin' there...

HAMLIN *drops the knife, finally breaking down in full tears.*

He furiously takes his hoodie off and throws it far away from him.

HAMLIN: I'm tryn' mum. I'm tryn'.

(*pause*)

HAMLIN: I'm so sorry.

MAMA H. *stand behind him heartbroken.*

HAMLIN *continues to undress slowly, taking off his new shoes and his watch.*

(*long beat*)

MAMA H. *helps a fragile* HAMLIN *back up and starts bringing him in the house, looking back, hoping to see* NIC. *She spots the transformer toy on the floor. She places it on the garden wall.*

Transition lights.

HAMLIN *is sitting near the table. His phone on it and on speaker mode.* MAMA H. *is right behind him.*

METROPOLITAN POLICE: Metropolitan Police, how can I help?

Lights out.

REQUIEM

A couple of days later. Early morning.

HAMLIN *is in a Secure Training Centre. Sitting in the middle of a bare room, waiting. In the background, sound of young boys chattering.*

MAMA H. *comes in holding a leafy and healthy sage pot with the* "Hamlin" *label on it. She places it in front of* HAMLIN, *who does not react. There is an embarrassing silence in the air.*

MAMA H *starts singing "Eyes on the Sparrow",off key, to break the ice.*

MAMA H:

I sing because I'm happy.

I sing because I'm free…

HAMLIN *surrenders and chuckles.*

MAMA H: He's one of the last sages standin'. Look how full and leafy this baby is. Almost like a fresh salad. It has grown real nice u knaw, outside in de sun, well, some sun.

(*pause*)

Maybe am not so bad at dis after all.

(*pause*)

Nan would always say "We all need healing from the outside to come in."

(*pause*)

It's funny the way plants are born kinda tender, but den get brittle and dry, just like men. Yep, you came outta my womb soft and supple and—

HAMLIN: I love you too, Mum...

(*pause*)

Even though I dun miss your singing, your sneezing and all de leaves flying in de house.

HAMLIN *and* MAMA H. *giggle.*

A sad silence lingers for a bit.

MAMA H: You okay? You know I got the Teacher Assisting job at the end?

(*beat*)

You doing well here? Keeping out of trouble?

HAMLIN: Yeah...

(*long silent beat*)

MAMA H: Oh, almost forgot—

MAMA H *collects a scrunched paper from her bag.*

MAMA H: Found this near the other pots when I was cleaning up. Thought you might want to keep it.

MAMA H. *hands the paper to* HAMLIN.

HAMLIN *unfolds it. It's* QUINN*'s sketch of himself.* HAMLIN *smiles and turns the paper around to make out the drawing.*

HAMLIN: Maybe he did look a bit like Idris... (*painfully laughs*) He deserved a proper send off.

MAMA H: There's no such thing as a proper send off. The spirit lives on. We eventually become bones and dirt—

HAMLIN: He wasn't... He wasn't dirt. He's clean now.

MAMA H: U gotta trust that he's resting in a better place. You said it best, "He now an Angel. Restin' somewhere quiet."

(*beat*)

You know Nic, he, well nobody knows where he is...

HAMLIN: Yeh...

From off stage an adult voice is heard.

YOUTH PRISON GUARD: Time's up.

MAMA H. *starts to leave, reluctantly.*

HAMLIN: Mum?

MAMA H: Yeh?

93

HAMLIN: I finally had a dream. A good one. I can finally say that.

(*pause*)

I was playin' in the ocean and heard some footsteps coming closer and closer. Quinn popped up right as I turned around.

(*pause*)

I called his name…

(*pause*)

…and he said: "What's-up?…what's up, Hamlin King."

A buzzing sound is heard in the background.

CURTAIN